Renovations

Carmel Reilly   Courtney Hopkinson

Nelson Thornes

Nelson Thornes

First published in 2007 by Cengage Learning Australia
www.cengage.com.au

This edition published under the imprint of Nelson Thornes Ltd,
Delta Place, 27 Bath Road, Cheltenham, United Kingdom, GL53 7TH

10 9 8 7 6 5 4 3 2
11 10 09 08

Renovations
ISBN 978-1-4085-0128-3

Story by Carmel Reilly
Illustrations by Courtney Hopkinson
Edited by Johanna Rohan
Designed by Vonda Pestana
Series Design by James Lowe
Production Controller Seona Galbally
Audio recordings by Juliet Hill, Picture Start
Spoken by Matthew King and Abbe Holmes
Printed in China by 1010 Printing International Ltd

Website www.nelsonthornes.com

Renovations

Carmel Reilly   Courtney Hopkinson

Contents

Chapter 1

BANG, BANG, BANG!

Jack woke to the sound of banging.
"What's going on?" he asked,
sitting up and rubbing his eyes.

BANG, BANG, BANG!

"Stop making that terrible noise, Jack,"
his mother called from downstairs.

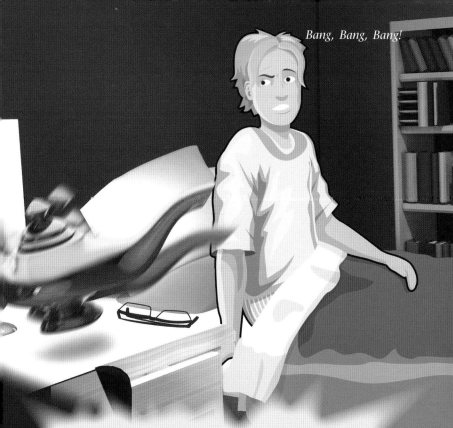

Bang, Bang, Bang!

Jack looked around his bedroom.
Then, he realised what was happening.

"Oh no!" he cried, leaping out of bed
and diving towards his desk.
He saved the lamp
from toppling off the edge
just in time.

Jack was the only person he knew
who had a magic lamp and a genie.

Gemini, the genie,
wasn't easy to get along with.

Gemini only gave Jack one wish a day,
and because he was grumpy
and played tricks,
Jack's wishes hardly ever came true.

As Jack rubbed the lamp
and waited for Gemini to appear,
he wondered what would happen
this time.

Bang, Bang, Bang!

Chapter 2

RENOVATING

"I'm busy.
What is it?" asked Gemini,
looking as grumpy as ever.

"I just wondered about the banging,"
Jack said.

"I'm renovating," said Gemini.

Jack shrugged.
"You'd better keep the noise down,
or Mum will find out about you."

Running Words 171

"Only the owner of the lamp
can see me, so I'll be safe.
But, you might get into trouble
for making too much noise,"
laughed Gemini,
disappearing in a puff of smoke.

Jack went downstairs for breakfast.
Just as he was about to eat,
there was a huge bang.

"What is that noise?"
asked his mum.

"It might be the cat," said Jack.

"Well, he's wearing very big boots," said Mum, as she raced upstairs.

Chapter 3

WHAT'S GOING ON?

"Jack!" yelled his mum,
from upstairs.
"Come here now!"
Jack ran to his bedroom.
"What's this?" she asked him.

12

Jack's mouth fell open.
His room was full of bricks,
and lots of dust.

"So?" said his mum, looking serious.
"What's going on?"

Jack thought quickly.

"Sorry, Mum," he said.

"That noise must have been
the bricks falling over.
I got them yesterday to make
a ... um ... a model."

Jack's mum gave him a strange look.

"I'd like to learn to build things," he said weakly.

"We have a garage for that," said his mum, shaking her head.

When his mum had gone,
Jack closed the door
and rubbed the lamp.

Gemini appeared,
shaking dust everywhere.
"What now?" Gemini asked.
"I said I was busy."

"I don't want all this mess
out here," said Jack.

Gemini took a deep breath.
"Where else am I going to put it?"
he asked Jack.

"Can't you wish it away?"
Jack asked.

Gemini looked at him and frowned. "It doesn't work like that," he said. "You're the one who makes the wishes around here. Not me."

Chapter 4

MAKING SOME CHANGES

Jack was about to wish the mess away when he realised something.

"You mean you can't make wishes for yourself?" he asked.

Gemini shook his head grumpily.

"So, I could make wishes for you?" asked Jack slowly.

"Yes," said Gemini, looking puzzled.

"Well, what if I help you
by wishing for your renovation?"
asked Jack.

"Why would you do that?"
asked Gemini.

"Because I'm a nice person,"
smiled Jack.

Gemini frowned at Jack.
"You want something in return,
don't you?"

Jack smiled.
"Well, sort of ..."

Jack made the wish,
and Gemini disappeared into his lamp.
Jack could hear laughing
and yelling from inside.

Finally, Gemini appeared again.
It was the first time Jack
had ever seen him really smile.

"My place looks wonderful!"
Gemini said.
Then, he looked serious.
"So, what is it you want in return?"

23

"I want you to stop being grumpy," said Jack.

Gemini frowned.
"I am never grumpy,"
he said grumpily.
Then he disappeared.

Jack heard a door slam
from inside the lamp.
He could see that some things
would never change.

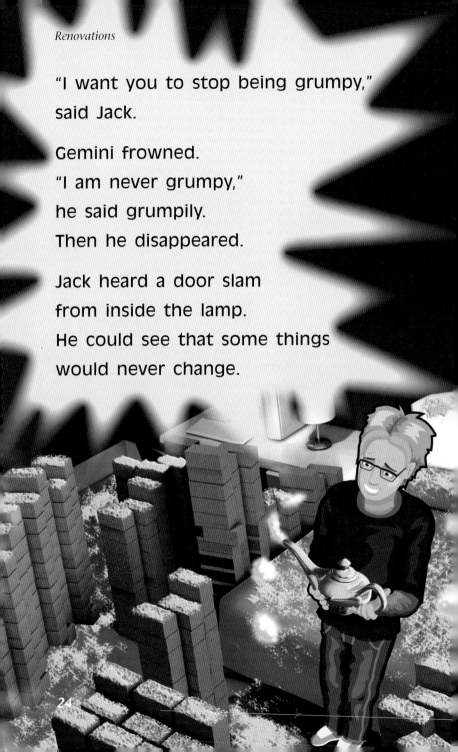